# THE
# Creepy, Crawly
# BOOK

by Bobbi Katz
illustrated by S.D. Schindler

W9-BBX-677

Learning Ladders/New York

Text copyright © 1989 by Random House, Inc.
Illustrations copyright © 1989 by S.D. Schindler.
All rights reserved under International and Pan-American Copyright Conventions.
Published in the United States by Random House, Inc., New York,
and simultaneously in Canada by Random House of Canada Limited, Toronto.
ISBN: 0-394-82709-0   Manufactured in Singapore   1 2 3 4 5 6 7 8 9 0

How many different kinds of animals can you name?
Did you forget about the biggest group of all—insects?
In fact, three out of every four animals are insects.
Unlike many other animals, insects don't have bones.
They have tough skin and strong muscles instead.

An adult insect has three main parts: the head,
thorax, and abdomen. To these three parts other parts,
such as feelers, wings, and legs, are attached.

feeler

There are more kinds of insects than all other kinds of animals and plants put together! There were insects on the earth even before there were dinosaurs. Some of them are probably creeping, crawling, or flying around your house or garden right now. Let's look.

wings

head

thorax

abdomen

legs

# How Do Insects Grow?

A baby elephant looks like a little elephant. A kitten looks like a little cat. You are clearly a little person. But many insects change so much while they are growing, they don't look anything like their parents. Some go through three stages. Others grow in four stages. The stages are the egg, larva, pupa, and adult.

eggs   larva   pupa   adult

**Egg:** Some insects lay eggs in nests, but others deposit them in sand, on leaves, in garbage, or in soft wood. Unlike most insects, the earwig guards her eggs until they hatch. Those pincers on the back of her body look vicious, but she probably only uses them in self-defense.

Put the earwig sticker near the earwig mother's eggs, nestled by that big rock.

**Larva:** In weeks or months larvae ooze out of their eggs. All of them are very hungry. First they gobble up their own egg cases. Then they keep on eating. And eating. Usually each kind of larva eats only one kind of food. Some eat anything—leaves, wood, feathers, manure, or even their own brothers and sisters!

Larvae wiggle along slowly. As they grow they shed their skins, changing their size and coloring. Lots of birds, and even other insects, think larvae taste good. Since they don't have wings to fly away from their enemies, most larvae don't become adults. That's a good thing! Otherwise insects would take over the world.

Put the lacewing larva sticker on a plant where it can find its favorite food—tiny insects called aphids.

**Pupa to Adult:** When larvae are big enough, they are ready for a long, magical rest. Some larvae burrow into the ground or into trees for their pupal snooze. Some grubs, or beetle larvae, spend several years as pupae. Other larvae settle down on a branch or fence. Then they spin a cocoon around themselves until they're completely covered. While they're inside, they change into adults.

When the insects finally break out of their coverings, they look like copies of their parents.

Butterflies hang upside down until their wings are hard enough to open. Place the sticker of the adult butterfly so that it seems to fly away from the monarch butterfly cocoon.

cocoon

# Swimmers and Divers

Ponds and lakes are dandy homes to all sorts of insects.
There are plenty of plants and animals to eat. Water
striders hurry along the surface. Water boatmen use
their long legs like oars and swim forward and
backward. Mosquito larvae and pupae live right at th
surface of the water. Their long hairs keep them
until they're ready to buzz off and bit

water strider

water bug

mosquito pupa

water boatman

Beautiful dragonflies live near ponds. Their fierce and ugly larvae shoot out powerful jaws to catch tadpoles, fish, and mosquitoes. Water bugs come in all sizes. Giant water bugs are water demons! Their long front legs have hooks for grabbing. Then ZAP—their sharp beaks send mild poison into whatever they catch. Next they use their beaks to suck out its blood or other body fluids.

What will the water bug on the sticker catch first? A tadpole, a fish, or even a frog?

## Musicians

Grasshoppers, crickets, and locusts belong to one of the most talented families in the insect world. These look-alikes are not only terrific jumpers, they also are musicians. Grasshoppers fiddle all summer long by drawing one of their legs across one of their wings.

Crickets make their chirping sound by rubbing their wings together. They live inside houses, so you might even hear one singing in your basement in the middle of winter.

Can you find a place to stick a cricket?

grasshopper

cricket

Locusts are big grasshoppers. Some years millions of them band together in swarms. What a deafening noise they make! And what a sight they are, flying off in search of more food after they have eaten up all the plants in one place. A swarm can be like a terrible summer blizzard. Add your own to the scene here.

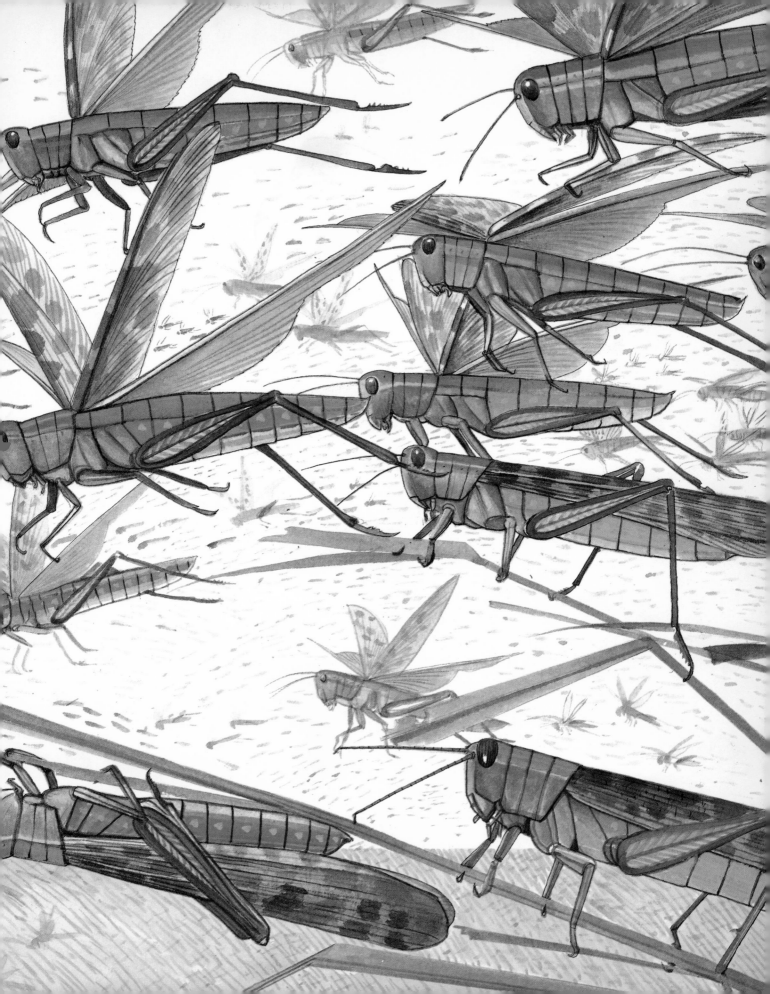

# Pests

Just about every plant you can think of has its own pest—an insect that feeds on it.

Beetles eat big plants and little plants.

Caterpillars destroy trees.

Moth larvae eat holes in your wool clothes.

Fleas bite your dog and cat.

Flies even come for supper
at your house.
What is the fly on your sticker
going to taste first?

## Pals

Have you ever had a really itchy mosquito bite? Did you ever find a worm in your apple? That makes it hard to think of insects as helpers, but they are. If you like honey, you'll agree that bees are terrific helpers. Bees use their own wax to build honeycombs in hollow trees. The honeycombs are full of tiny separate rooms called cells. The queen bee lays eggs in some cells. Worker bees fill other cells with nectar from flowers. As bees gather nectar they carry dusty pollen on their hairy bodies and fly from one flower to another. The plants bees visit will make more seeds or fruit.

Put the sticker of the honeybee near the queen bee.

## Night Visitors

At twilight you can see insects that you don't notice during the day.

Moths come out. Even though their wings are shaped like those of brightly colored butterflies, their dull colors help them disappear during the daytime.

Fireflies' blinking lights glow in the dark. Something called luciferin causes them to light up. Some fireflies lay eggs that glow in the dark. Their larvae are glowworms. Fireflies flash lights to signal to each other. If you catch fireflies, don't keep them in a closed jar too long. They need more air than other beetles.

As you lie in bed listen to the songs of all the night insects. They are a summer's orchestra. Before you close the book, put the moth sticker near the lantern.